The BACKBONE Solution:
Eight Adjustments to Strengthen
the Core of Your Workplace Email

Cathy McKee Dees, PhD
Lynna Garber Kalna

Paula,
I will still like
you even if I find
this book in the
y me a Locker room!
Best,
Cathy

Cover Design and Layout
Diana Puppin, dp Impact Marketing & Design, Cincinnati, OH
www.dpImpactMarketing.com

Paperback: ISBN: 978-0-578-39090-1

Ebook ISBN: 978-0-578-39091-8

Disclaimer: All references to persons or organizations used expressly as examples are fictional; any resemblance to real persons or organizations is unintentional.

Dees/Kalna Press

"You've read them, you've written them, and now with The BACKBONE Solution you can master crafting emails that capture your recipients' attention, interest, and desired action. The authors share how to write less and deliver more. Although their focus is how to write more effective and compelling emails, their tutorials will sharpen all of your written communications."

Jay Jacobs, Biggest Loser Season 11 Final 4 Alumni, TEDx Speaker, Author

Lynna Kalna has a unique balance of experience in the academic and corporate worlds. She is a masterful business communicator, passionate about the power of communication, and skilled in designing and delivering training programs for companies, educational institutions, and professional organizations. She is co-author of **The Write Direction: A New Teacher's Practical Guide to Teaching Writing and Its Application to the Workplace.** Lynna has focused her career on helping people develop their communication edge—to stand out, be heard, and get the job done.

Cathy Dees is an expert educator and corporate trainer specializing in business communication. She is co-author of **The Writer's Handbook for College and Career** and is passionate about the evolution of language and how it is used in business and professional writing. Her experience in higher education, business, and non-profit organizations provides Cathy with a broad background that allows her to create comprehensive communication training loaded with moxie—spunk, confidence, and skill.

Contents

Introduction

Written information is everywhere—you can't avoid it. Even with super-convenient technology such as a webinar in the palm of your hand, you're still going to end up writing.

We transact most business using some form of written communication, and more often than not, email is involved. In fact, in the workplace, email is **the** core communication channel—the virtual solar plexus for building relationships, distributing information, and solving problems. Nonetheless, people often avoid addressing issues regarding the communication health of their email messages; they realize something is wrong, but just as they avoid going to the doctor, they really don't want to know what their communication ailments are.

Frequently, writing an email, which is familiar and essential to workplace operations, is uncomfortable and time consuming. Why? Well, in addition to having to learn incessant updates to communication technology, many people just haven't been adequately trained when it comes to writing effective email messages.

Welcome to the Workplace Email Clinic

Do you have writing insurance? Well, yes, you do—this book! It's just the insurance you need to create workplace emails that crush communication wellness checks and preventive screenings—no premiums, no deductibles.

Let's triage. Where does it hurt? Your back—from bending over backward to get your workplace messages understood correctly? Your wrist—from looking at your watch and wondering why you're spending so much time writing and managing so many freaking emails?

What workplace email treatments have you considered? Dancing around naked under a full moon? Creative. Seeking advice from a psychic? Unreliable. Or maybe less dramatic interventions such as trying to follow a poorly written style guide? Frustrating. Taking a course? Expensive. Googling suggestions? Overwhelming.

We get it. So, we developed the BACKBONE solution, a systematic approach to improving the health, strength, and posture of your workplace email. Designed for professionals at any level, in any kind of organization, it offers quick and easy strategies for building your email moxie. And while especially important to the routine email messages you write every day, these strategies also apply to all kinds of workplace writing. Basically, the BACKBONE

1

adjustments help you produce emails that work; think of these adjustments as your personalized treatment plan for workplace writing.

The Painful Reality of Email

Email is the lifeline that advances business goals and generates revenue . . . or not. It depends.

Email can either support circulation of robust, business-building messages or block vital communication pathways. Well-written emails facilitate the smooth flow of information to readers who need that information to take action. Poorly written messages clog communication arteries with verbal plaque that not only impedes communication but could ultimately kill business opportunities.

Therefore, in some situations, the consequences of poorly written emails can be serious: derailed careers, ruined reputations, reduced revenue. In fact, as of 2017, poor writing was costing American businesses nearly $400 billion per year.[1] Yikes! And, as you can see from the following examples, being careless with email isn't worth the risk:

- The CEO of Cerner Corporation sent a scathing email message to his employees berating them for not caring about the company and threatening them with layoffs and hiring freezes. The email was leaked, causing concern among analysts and investors. The result? Cerner's stock plummeted 22 percent in three days.[2]

- General Motors produced several car models that had documented ignition switch failures. The problem wasn't taken seriously because the issue was referenced in internal written correspondence as a "customer convenience" issue instead of a "safety defect." The result? Fatalities.[3]

And although most messages may not have the potential to elicit such serious

---

[1] Swystun, J. (2017, January 9). *The High Cost of Poor Writing*. Thinkgrowth.Org. Retrieved September 7, 2018, from https://thinkgrowth.org/the-high-cost-of-poor-writing-about-400-billion-559e9fe5f735

[2] Wong, E. (2001, April 5). *Stinking office memo boomerangs*. Https://Www.Nytimes. Com/2001/04/05/Business/Stinging-Office-Memo-Boomerangs-Chief-Executive-Criticized-after-Upbraiding.Html. Retrieved November 2, 2018, from https://www. nytimes.com/2001/04/05/business/stinging-office-memo-boomerangs-chief-executive-criticized-after-upbraiding.html

[3] Greg Gardner, Detroit Free Press. (2015, May 4). *GM ignition switch deaths rise to 97*. Detroit Free Press. Retrieved July 4, 2019, from https://eu.freep.com/story/money/2015/05/04/general-motors-ignition-deaths/26864231/

consequences, poorly written emails can cause damage by alienating, confusing, or demoralizing readers. Let's say you receive the following sales meeting message:

> *Our sales numbers are horrible. Due to horrible numbers, you are encouraged to attend a meeting in September 22 to get on the right track as it relates to improve sales revenue. Due to low sales numbers, we may not be reducing commision percentages. But, we need a new strategy. Make sure you come with an out-of-the-box strategy or the curtain may drop!*

Huh?

- Is the message easy to read and professional?
  You: Uh, no.
- Do you feel motivated, upbeat, and positive about this meeting?
  You: No!
- Is the meeting mandatory or optional?
  You: Mandatory. No, wait. Optional . . . I think.
- Do you feel alienated, confused, or demoralized?
  You: Actually, all three.
- Is your commission percentage being reduced?
  You: I guess so, but I'm not sure.

That email has several communication disorders: lacks clarity, offends readers, and includes mistakes. So frustrating! And messages like that one, with common afflictions such as spineless spelling or constipated construction, are time consuming and painful for readers. Don't be *that* writer.

Think of email as the communication muscle of business. And muscular email messages need a powerful, centralized core—a strong communication backbone—around which to develop. Align and strengthen your email backbone; then watch as you and your messages become more confident, more energetic, and more influential. Be *that* writer!

Your BACKBONE Workout

The BACKBONE adjustments are your painless guide to resuscitating your email writing practices and generating powerfully influential messages. Use these professional and practical strategies to create messages that are

- **B**icentric—centered on purpose and audience
- **A**ssertive—confident and positive

3

- **C**lear—easy to read and understand
- **K**een—sharp and precise
- **B**uff—concise and to the point
- **O**rdered—logically organized
- **N**ourished—complete and supplemented
- **E**rror Free—correct and accurate

Check out the sales meeting email after the BACKBONE adjustments:

> *Even with your hard work last quarter, sales are down 19%. So, to explore new sales strategies, I have scheduled a required meeting from 1:00-3:00 p.m. on Thursday, September 22 in conference room A. Please note that, currently, your commission percentage will remain the same.*
> *I look forward to a creative and robust discussion!*

Ahhh . . . so much better.

- Is the message easy to read and professional?
  You: Yup.

- Do you feel motivated, upbeat, and positive about this meeting?
  You: Why, yes, I do!

- Is the meeting mandatory or optional?
  You: Mandatory.

- Do you feel alienated, confused, or demoralized?
  You: No, I feel like part of the team.

- Is your commission percentage being reduced?
  You: Not right now.

Your Communication Chiropractor

Writing may feel complicated and frustrating. But if you think writing has to be painful, think again. Just because technology has made all of us writers all the time, writing doesn't need to cause chronic pain.

To ease your discomfort, each chapter in this book contains writing prescriptions. Additionally, the end of each chapter offers a short demonstration of BACKBONE adjustments in action: you'll see how to scan for and fix common problem areas.

So sit up in your chair—or pony up to that fancy ergonomic, stand-up desk—and start using the BACKBONE adjustments to write spectacular workplace emails. Not only will you understand how to improve messages already drafted, you'll also write better messages from the start. Plus, you'll have the spunk, confidence, and skill to

- Increase the speed of your email writing and communication processes.
- Write messages readers can easily understand and act on.
- Reduce the number of email messages you send and receive.

Professional Protocols

Before we explain the BACKBONE adjustments in detail, here are a few general guidelines regarding standards for professional communication.

Ethical and Legal Considerations

- Be honest, transparent, authentic, and complete in your business communication.
- Know the current communication laws and regulations that govern your industry.
- Seek advice from your legal team or HR department for guidance, if needed.
- Remember, an email stays in the system even if you click "Delete."

Communication Practices

- Select the appropriate messaging channel—make sure email is the best way to communicate the message before you write and send it.
- Be mindful of when to use "Reply All," "cc," and "bcc."
- Use your out-of-office auto reply when you won't be reading messages (and remember to turn it off when you return to work).
- Respond to emails within 24 hours (or about one business day).
- Be aware of emotionally charged situations—avoid initiating or responding to them via email. Use a different medium.

Use these protocols in conjunction with the BACKBONE adjustments to identify your email aches and pains and to learn how to improve your communication habits. You'll be writing brawny emails, painlessly, in no time.

Trust us. Your life as a writer is about to get a lot easier.

Bicentric

The first core BACKBONE adjustment is bicentric. Something that's bicentric has **two central components**, what we like to call driving factors. Think of a bicycle—two wheels working together, in sync, to propel you forward. A bicycle is driven by your power and helps you accomplish their purpose of getting where you want to go. To get your email messages to accomplish their purpose, harness the synergy of the **two central components** of any workplace message: purpose (your goal) and audience (the reader).

A workplace email that's bicentric has two priorities: clearly communicating its goal (accomplishing its purpose) with an awareness of the reader's needs (attention to audience). Granted, determining purpose and analyzing audience are easier with some messages than with others. A bicentric email gets business done because it contains the proper information based on its purpose AND because it's written with the reader in mind. So how can you write messages that are bicentric?

Strategies

1. Determine Your Purpose

You know you need to write a message. But since a message's purpose dictates its content and organization, you'll accomplish your goal more effectively if

7

you first understand the overall purpose of the message, such as to extend an invitation, reject a proposal, or suggest an idea. Usually, the purpose fits into one of three general categories: positive/neutral, negative, or persuasive.

Positive/Neutral

- Request/share information
- Make an announcement
- Convey congratulations
- Build goodwill

For example, if your goal is to invite employees to a company picnic, then your email will be a positive/neutral message to share information.

Negative

- Deny a request
- Convey bad news
- Refuse an offer
- Register a complaint

For example, if your goal is to let an employee steering committee know that the company won't implement its requested flextime options, then your email will be a negative message denying the request.

Persuasive

- Convince the reader to accept an idea or belief
- Motivate the reader to take action

For example, if your goal is to ask employees to donate unused sick days to an injured colleague, then your email will be persuasive, convincing them to contribute their available PTO.

If you aren't certain about your purpose, or goal, for sending a message, don't write it—yet. Why? A message without a clear purpose can wander all over the place, leaving your readers confused. Conversely, understanding your purpose guides you to create a message that's organized appropriately, includes relevant content, and motivates readers to embrace your goal. Remember, you're ready to write when, and only when, you know your goal.

Speaking of readers, the audience is the other equally important aspect of any bicentric workplace email. Just who are those mysterious people on the other end of "Send"?

2. Analyze Your Audience

The owners of the email addresses in the "To" field are **the** most important people; they ultimately determine whether your message accomplishes its purpose. You must plan how to connect with your audience relative to the topic of, and purpose for, a given message. Think of this plan as a quick, observational assessment that yields an overall summary—a general reader *profile* so to speak—of your readers' general interests and needs.

To create this basic reader profile

- Characterize your relationship to them, such as internal, external, colleague, superior, etc.

- Consider their knowledge of the topic, such as technical, nontechnical, familiar, unfamiliar, etc.

- Determine what information they need in order to act, such as background knowledge, context, content, etc.

- Predict their possible reactions, such as pleased, indifferent, angry, neutral, etc.

Because understanding your readers' perspectives is your key to communicating successfully, try your best to obtain this information. You'll want to develop a general awareness of your readers through actual knowledge, information, or observations rather than through reliance on uninformed, oversimplified, or prejudiced opinions about a particular person or group.

When you already know your readers, audience analysis will be quick. But take time to analyze unknown readers—a wise investment likely to help you accomplish your purpose while also building goodwill.

Use a snapshot analysis of your readers to figure out how they might react to your message. Then design that message—by adjusting content (what you say and in what order) and language (how you say it)—so it kindly and professionally guides your readers toward the reaction you want them to have.

Risks/Consequences

Not focusing on your purpose and your audience can cause critical message failure. For example, if your purpose isn't clear, your readers may not understand what the point is, what they're supposed to do, or even why the message should be important to them.

If readers feel like you're not really writing to them (have not considered their needs or interests), your message won't keep their attention. They won't read to the end and, thus, won't even know what you're offering or requesting. In that case, nothing happens. Everybody loses.

Also, if you fail to consider your audience's point of view, you most likely won't make a genuine connection. It's tough to get business done without positive and productive relationships. Further, if you haven't analyzed your readers, you risk frustrating or offending them. Even worse, you might convey the image that you're an insensitive communicator.

Email Situation

Chris emails his supervisor, Abby, requesting money to attend a conference:

TO: Abby Shultz
FROM: Chris Martinez
DATE: September 30, 2022
SUBJECT: Request to Attend Conference

Hi Abby,

I appreciate that our company provides funds for employees' professional development every year.

As part of my professional development and to prepare for our impending software updates, I'd like to attend this year's We're Wired IT conference in Denver, November 12-14. Total costs, including conference registration, transportation, accommodations, and meals, will be $1800.

So that I can meet the registration deadline, please let me know by October 10 if you can approve this request.

I'm excited about the opportunity to attend this conference so that I can ensure a smooth software transition.

Thanks,
Chris

Chris Martinez
Manager, Information Technology
DK Solutions
444.555.4343 // Direct

Abby writes a reply, and being the great communicator that she is, she scans the message before she clicks "Send." The purpose of scanning is to identify problem areas, related to the BACKBONE components, that may be limiting the message's effectiveness.

Bicentric Scan

To start the scanning procedure, Abby assesses her message's bicentric qualities—focusing on how well the message attends to purpose and audience. Take a look at how this works by examining Abby's email draft; pay special attention to the highlighted sections.

Misaligned Message with Bicentric Diagnosis

TO: Chris Martinez
FROM: Abby Shultz
DATE: October 1, 2022
SUBJECT: RE: Request to Attend Conference

Hi Chris,

I'm glad you'd like to attend the *We're Wired* IT conference. [expresses no general understanding of why Chris is interested in attending the conference]

Because we encourage employees' continuing education, our department budgeted $10K for professional development in 2022. I'm not sure if we can find enough money to cover the cost of the *We're Wired* conference. [doubtful phrasing doesn't make clear if Chris's conference request has been approved]

I'd be glad to discuss alternatives such as [lacks acknowledgement of the urgent importance to Chris, which is to help him get information for updating company software programs]
- Attending the virtual option of the *We're Wired* conference
- Completing a vendor-provided online training program
- Securing the remaining conference costs from other sources listed in the <u>HR Professional Development</u> folder

Let me know by October 5 if you'd like to meet to discuss your options. Or maybe we can work something out so you can actually attend the conference. [implies that if Chris argues his point, Abby might be open to funding the conference costs, which isn't the case]

Thanks for taking initiative regarding your continuing professional development.

Best,
Abby

Abby Shultz, PMP
Director of Operations
DK Solutions
444.555.4321 // Direct

Bicentric Adjustments

Notice how Abby's bicentric adjustments make the message's purpose clear and tailor the message to the reader.

Properly Aligned Message with Bicentric Adjustments

TO: Chris Martinez
FROM: Abby Shultz
DATE: October 1, 2022
SUBJECT: RE: Request to Attend Conference

Hi Chris,

I appreciate your interest in attending the *We're Wired* IT conference—staying current in our industry is important to both your professional development and our department's goals. *[demonstrates awareness of Chris's interest in professional development as well as his desire to obtain current information needed for his job]*

Because we encourage employees' continuing education, our department budgeted $10K for professional development in 2022. However, due to the high volume of applications and approvals since January, only $500 remains available. *[pays attention to purpose by specifically stating that only $500 remains for professional development]*

I'd be glad to discuss alternatives that would help you prepare for the software updates *[validates awareness of Chris's most obvious reasons for wanting to attend this conference]* such as
- Attending the virtual option of the *We're Wired* conference
- Completing a vendor-provided online training program
- Securing the remaining conference costs from other sources listed in the <u>HR Professional Development</u> folder

I want to make sure we secure that $500 for you; so, let me know by October 5 if you'd like to meet to discuss your options. *[states an action item with a deadline]*

Thanks for taking initiative regarding your continuing professional development.

Best,
Abby

Abby Shultz, PMP
Director of Operations
DK Solutions
444.555.4321 // Direct

Observe how these changes better align the message so that Abby's purpose is accomplished and her awareness of the reader is evident. You, too, can decrease possible pain points and increase your chances of success if you revise your emails by making bicentric adjustments.

Use your business writing backbone to make sure your messages are bicentric—stick to the point (your purpose) and focus on the most important person (your audience). These two elements are the driving factors for everything you write—they support and influence each of the other components of the BACKBONE adjustments.

To help you keep track of the adjustments throughout the book, use the checklist at the end of each chapter. The complete checklist is in the Appendix.

BACKBONE Adjustments: What to Check Before You Click "Send"

• Purpose—clearly stated and focused
• Audience—attends to reader's needs and possible reactions

Assertive

Assertive

A large part of customizing an email is making sure the message has an appropriate tone. In writing, tone is the emotional atmosphere that surrounds what's said in a message; it's the part of the message that conveys meaning beyond the actual words. Tone is the written equivalent to, "It's not what you said; it's how you said it."

Although there are many effective tones for communicating (as well as tones to avoid), you'll always be more successful in accomplishing your purpose if your tone is assertive.

Wimpy or Assertive?

To illustrate, let's say you're being interviewed for a job. What impression would you make if you did the following during a face-to-face or virtual interview?

- Wore a one-size-fits-all bright green plaid suit
- Stared at your shoes and answered questions with "um" and "uh"
- Waited for the interviewer to ask the right questions about your selling points
- Responded with negativity and complaints about past experiences

How would the impression you make be different if you did the following, instead?

- Wore appropriate, well-fitting attire
- Displayed confident, friendly body language and facial expressions
- Maintained eye contact
- Answered questions with responses that showed preparation, self-knowledge, positive attitude, and focus on the goal

We don't need to tell you the answers. You already know. But what's just as important as how you conduct yourself at an interview is how you construct and deliver your written communication. Just like a person entering a room conveys a style and makes an impression, an email message also conveys a style and makes an impression; consequently, the tone of your writing affects the way readers interpret and respond to your message and to you. So how can you control the tone of your writing?

Tone and style refer to how something is written—the words you select, the phrasing (the way words are grouped together), and the punctuation you choose. These all work together to generate an impression. For example, which would you prefer to read?

1. *If you aren't able to understand the information for the proposal, I can go over the steps again.*

2. *I'm happy to help you organize the information for the proposal.*

Even though these two sentences communicate roughly the same thought, the first example gives the impression the writer thinks the reader isn't very smart; the second sentence conveys a tone that makes the writer seem helpful, friendly, and approachable. That's the power of tone.

So, like a prepared and self-assured interviewee, assertive writing

- Employs an effective tone: sets an appropriate emotional atmosphere around what's being communicated—it dresses well and enters the room with a smile.
- Emits confidence: conveys certainty and sincerity—it arrives prepared and ready to speak.

Strategies

The challenge in business writing is twofold: to communicate the message and to communicate it in the optimal way. To make sure your emails are communicated in the best, most assertive manner, use the following five strategies.

1. **Use Positive Words and Phrasing to Develop a Positive Tone**

When you use positive words and phrases, you're more likely to achieve your objective and build goodwill for you and your company.

- Words can have denotative (dictionary) as well as connotative (emotional) meanings. So, choose words carefully. Take the word *clique*, for example. In a dictionary, it's defined as a group of persons. But it also conjures negative connotations as being an exclusive group of self-serving people that excludes outsiders. Note what using the word *clique* implies: *the clique in the sales department* vs. *the team in the sales department*. We'd rather meet with the "team" in the sales department!

- Use positive words rather than negative words. Avoid using negative trigger words such as *no, not, sorry, regret, unfortunately, never, difficult, neglect, failure, delay, sadly, complaint, issue*, and *problem*. For example, in a subject line, instead of *Delay in the Spencer Project*, make your subject line more positive: *Changes in the Spencer Project*. Examples in a message:

Negative: *Don't forget to send a Zoom link to the participants.*

Positive: *Remember to send a Zoom link to the participants.*

Negative: *Your order has been delayed because you failed to include the expiration date for your credit card.*

Positive: *We will ship your order as soon as we receive your credit card's expiration date.*

2. **Tell People What Can Be Done Rather Than What Can't Be Done**

Nothing can be gained by telling people what they can't do or what you can't do. Instead, focus on what can be done. For example, *We will send a representative on Monday, May 8* is more positive than, *We cannot send a representative until Monday, May 8*. Emphasize the solution rather than the problem.

3. **Be Courteous and Sincere**

If you're respectful and honest, readers are more likely to accept your message, even a bad news message. So, avoid words and phrases that make you sound insincere, such as *To be honest* and catchphrases such as *Don't go there*.

And when appropriate, remember to include *please* and *thank you*, but not *thank you in advance*, which can seem a bit presumptuous.

4. **Be Confident—Assertive, Not Passive or Aggressive**

Look at the following three examples from cover letters where the writer is requesting an interview:

If something would come available that you think I might be qualified for and it wouldn't be too much trouble, please contact me at 555-555-5555.

This first example basically says, "Hey, I'm a schlep. You know it; I know it. But if a position becomes available and you think, oh, what the heck, and you happen to have my number handy and five minutes to kill, give me a call."

I will be at your office Monday morning for an interview. Please make sure you are in your office.

This second example crosses the line: it's arrogant and aggressive, implying, "You're interviewing me for this job on Monday, and you'll do it whenever I get there." That's not going to go over very well with the reader!

I'll be calling you early next week to see if we can set up a mutually convenient time for an interview. I'm excited to meet with you to discuss how I can contribute to your department.

The underlying message in this third example is, "I'm confident about my abilities and what I can contribute to your company. Let's get together. I think you'll be impressed." This is the confident tone you want!

5. Know What Tones to Avoid and How to Avoid Them

Some common negative tones to avoid are blunt, angry, sarcastic, fault-finding, preachy, and condescending. Also avoid being cutesy or too flowery. And to eliminate a doubtful tone in your messages, stay away from beginning sentences with *I think, I feel, I trust, If you agree,* and similar self-conscious terms. Furthermore, eliminate long-winded, wallowing apologies. If you've made a mistake, write a one-sentence apology and use the rest of the paragraph to explain how you'll rectify the situation.

Unprofessional tones interfere with the reception of your messages. Imagine what might result if you did any of the following:

- Imply your audience is stupid: *If you had read the directions correctly* . . . .
- Suggest your audience is lying: *You claimed you had contacted us* . . . .
- Blame your audience: *Obviously, you neglected to* . . . .

Fine-tuning the tone of your email can be tricky because there's not just one right way to craft a message—tone is subjective and can be interpreted differently by different readers. When writing or revising, be mindful of what your tone and style might be implying and how various readers might infer something different from the same message based on how you say it.

And with some messages, before you click "Send," it helps to have some cooling off time—emotional distance from the message, the reader, and/or the subject. You might be shocked at the tone of some of your emails once you read them an hour or two after the heat of the moment. Another good idea is to ask a colleague to give you feedback on a message before you send it. No amount of "oops" will fix sending a message that says, *That was not our mistake, and there's nothing more we can do.* Avoid the dreaded next-day, gut-wrenching affliction—"Crap, I should have re-written that."

Risks/Consequences

The consequences of not being assertive in your business communication are significant and far reaching. For one, you may be misunderstood and, therefore, not accomplish your purpose.

In addition, if your messages exude wimpishness, readers may get the impression you're a pushover, an appeaser, or someone who sends mixed messages because you can't say no or deliver bad news. At the other extreme, if your messages ooze backhanded aggressiveness, readers may feel bullied—shoved rather than nudged.

Most of us have received emails we've found upsetting, inappropriate, or curt. As a writer, creating the right tone can mean the difference between offending your reader and building a professional relationship. Consequently, it can be the difference between getting what you want, being ignored, or spending precious time fixing damage.

Overall, poor tone in your emails can cause communication gaps that escalate into misunderstandings, resentment, and frustration.

Assertive Scan

For this BACKBONE component, Abby assesses the message for its assertive qualities—focusing on tone, the attitude conveyed throughout the message.

Misaligned Message with Assertive Diagnosis

TO: Chris Martinez
FROM: Abby Shultz
DATE: October 1, 2022
SUBJECT: RE: Request to Attend Conference Denied *[negative wording]*

Hi Chris,

I appreciate your interest in attending the *We're Wired* IT conference—staying current in our industry is important to both your professional development and our department's goals.

Because we encourage employees' continuing education, our department budgeted $10K for professional development in 2022. However, I regret to inform you *[negative wording]* that we cannot fully fund your conference attendance *[tells Chris what can't be done]*. We only have $500 remaining, so there's no way we can cover the costs of attending the conference. Other possible funding sources are listed in the HR Professional Development folder. *[is vague about what can be done]*

I hope this won't discourage you from *[lack of confidence and negative phrasing]* continuing your professional development.

Better luck next time. *[sounds sarcastic rather than sincere]*

Best,

Abby

Abby Shultz, PMP
Director of Operations
DK Solutions
444.555.4321 // Direct

Assertive Adjustments

Notice how Abby improves the tone of this message with some assertive adjustments.

Properly Aligned Message with Assertive Adjustments

TO: Chris Martinez
FROM: Abby Shultz
DATE: October 1, 2022
SUBJECT: RE: Request to Attend Conference *[omits negative "denied"]*

Hi Chris,

I appreciate your interest in attending the *We're Wired* IT conference—staying current in our industry is important to both your professional development and our department's goals.

Because we encourage employees' continuing education, our department budgeted $10K for professional development in 2022. However, due to the high volume of applications and approvals since January, only $500 remains available. *[states bad news in less negative terms]*

I'd be glad to discuss alternatives *[tells what can be done rather than what can't be done]* that would help you prepare for the software updates such as
- Attending the virtual option of the We're Wired conference
- Completing a vendor-provided online training program
- Securing the remaining conference costs from other sources listed in the HR Professional Development folder

I want to make sure we secure that $500 for you; so, let me know by October 5 if you'd like to meet to discuss your options. *[shows confidence and assertive attitude]*

Thanks for taking initiative regarding your continuing professional development. *[uses positive wording]*

Best,
Abby

Abby Shultz, PMP
Director of Operations
DK Solutions
444.555.4321 // Direct

Abby knows that when she writes, she communicates an attitude as well as a message. Her assertive adjustments communicate the message to Chris with a more positive tone.

Instead of arriving at work and mindlessly sending out or replying to emails, use good judgement and set the right tone for every message. Put yourself in the readers' shoes, and consider the message from their viewpoints. Finessing your writing so it has a confident style and a positive vibe is key to building and maintaining strong relationships, projecting a professional image, and achieving your purpose.

Seek opportunities to improve your business acumen by devising and following a plan to move forward, assertively, via messages that are confidently and positively styled and effectively phrased.

BACKBONE Adjustments: What to Check Before You Click "Send"

• Tone—positive words and phrasing; states what can be done
• Style—confident, courteous, and sincere

Clear

Clear

A message that isn't clear can cause all kinds of breakdowns in communication. Imagine your readers as drivers heading north along Highway 1 toward San Francisco. Thick fog rolls in, and they aren't sure about the road ahead. Drivers can't see curves or signs and aren't sure where their exit is. To avoid an accident, they pull over and stop. Don't make your readers do the same thing—pull over and stop reading—when they receive a message from you.

Like drivers, readers need to see where they're going. Readers shouldn't have to guess what you're trying to say. Nor should they have to work hard to navigate through a message that's basically a three-paragraph pile-up of verbal chaos. And they don't have time to wait until the communication fog lifts. They're busy people who want to understand your main point quickly and easily.

Rather than liter the communication freeway with linguistic fender benders and confused readers, make sure your writing is clear. Clarity is the road map to effective writing. For the other BACKBONE components to have any meaning at all, your writing must be clear.

Clear emails meet the following criteria:

- Are easy to read, follow, and understand

    Foggy example:

23

The personal opinion of this writer is that when deadlines have the characteristics of negotiation, they are no longer effective.

Clear example:

Negotiable deadlines are ineffective.

- Have one clear meaning

  Write so there's only one way to interpret your message, unlike the unintentionally kinky ad that stated a three-piece set of mixing bowls "... was designed to please a cook with a round bottom for efficient beating." Or this ad about a dog for adoption: " ... a 10-week-old Spitz mix female and will grow to be medium sized. She does well inside. Sterilization is mandatory for anyone wanting to take her."

Strategies

You've identified your purpose in sending your email and have considered the needs and expectations of your audience. Now you can apply strategies to make your message even more clear.

1. Be Selective in Your Word Choice

- Choose words appropriate for the reader and the context. For example, with a professional audience, don't use emojis (😊) and text speak (LMK). And use, with discretion, acronyms (words made from the first letter of each word in a phase, such as *FEMA* for Federal Emergency Management Agency) and initialisms (letters pronounced individually that represent the first letter of each word in a phrase, such as *FBI* for Federal Bureau of Investigation). Additionally, make sure your audience is familiar with any industry-specific jargon you use.

- Use familiar words. Those fancy words you find in that handy thesaurus app could negatively impact message clarity, making reading difficult or causing misunderstanding. Big words just make you sound pretentious and arrogant. The focus of your writing should be to convey a clear message to your reader, the person who needs to understand your message. The purpose of an email is not to demonstrate the extent of your vocabulary.

Recognize the power of everyday, conversational words.

Foggy: *Our company experienced a fourth-quarter equity retreat.*

Clear: *Our company lost 10% in revenues during the fourth quarter.*

2. Improve the Clarity of Your Sentences

- ### Avoid Awkwardness

  Write the way you talk. Make your writing "sound" like you're speaking conversationally in your best professional voice *to that particular reader, in that particular situation.* Instead of writing business messages in the super-casual language you might use with your pals at the local gym, *Run this pro dev op by your people and see what the push-back is,* write the way you normally talk in workplace situations, such as, *Please tell your employees about this professional development opportunity and let me know their response.*

  Additionally, before clicking "Send," you can reduce awkwardness by slowly reading your message out loud, rather than skimming through it silently (like so many people do). Try it—you'll be amazed! No, really. Reading out loud gives you a different perspective. And that different perspective provides objectivity, which helps you notice mistakes.

- ### Keep Sentences Short

  It's not a mortal sin to have a sentence that exceeds 20 words, but to make your emails more understandable and easier to read, the majority of your sentences should be fewer than 20 words. Short sentences are more easily digested. If you try to pack too many words into one sentence, your reader may end up with a vowel obstruction.

- ### Develop Fluency

  To aid the readability, as well as improve the clarity of your messages, vary your sentence structure and use transitions.

  Avoid several short, choppy sentences that are all in subject-verb-object order. We know—we just told you to keep your sentences short, but don't take it to an extreme.

  ### Choppy

  This is a short sentence. I've added another sentence. I think a short sentence is fine. Some people don't. They think several short sentences back to back become boring.

  You can see and practically hear the choppy monotony.

Fluent

This is a short sentence. However, I've added another sentence and combined them, so that short sentence is fine. Several short sentences back to back become monotonous; therefore, vary your sentence structure.

Obviously, you can improve the readability of your email messages by varying your sentence types, openings, and length.

Also, use transitions that consist of single words, phrases, or a sentence. Transitions are the connective tissues that hold the skeleton of your business writing together because they help readers understand connections between your ideas. For example, transitions can be used to

- Continue or shift a line of thought, such as *also* or *however*
- Establish a sequence or time frame, such as *next* or *finally*
- Indicate examples or show emphasis, such as *to illustrate* or *on the positive side*

3. Incorporate Basic Design Techniques

Before your audience even reads your message, they get an impression about you and the message itself. Characteristics such as font size, style, and line spacing can make or break the success of the message. A message's initial impression impacts readers' attitudes.

- Paragraph Length: As a general guideline, paragraphs in your email should be no more than seven lines. And, feel free to use a one-sentence paragraph, which is an effective technique to highlight a point and to aid clarity. Remember that the point of a sentence is to convey a single thought, and the point of a paragraph is to convey an idea. So, if one sentence clearly conveys a complete idea, then it can be a paragraph. Sidenote: Paragraphs are not indented in an email, so remember to leave a blank line between paragraphs.
- Graphic Highlighting: One of the best ways to enhance the appearance of your email and to improve readability is to incorporate graphic highlighting techniques, such as

  - Bulleted, numbered, or lettered lists
  - Underline, boldface type, italics, and color
  - Headings and subheadings

Bulleted lists work best for related items when their order doesn't matter. Numbered or lettered lists work best when order or sequence is important or when items in the list are referred to later in the message. Just make sure your list has a properly punctuated lead-in sentence and is written in parallel form (i.e., each item starts with the same kind of word, such as a present-tense verb, noun, etc.).

Read this message and try to figure out what you need to do:

Our HR department has designed a program encouraging employees to use public transportation when going to and from work. The first step employees should take involves determining if mass transit is available where they live and which transit system they'll use. The second thing they should do is read the Commuter Reimbursement Plan (available on the company portal) to understand the plan's financial benefits and to decide how they would like to be reimbursed. Next, they should sign up for the program, offered through AD Systems, and select which options on the form are applicable for them. Finally, all three forms should be filed through the company portal. It is important that employees check the boxes on the last form, indicating how they want to be reimbursed.

Did you even read all that? We understand if you didn't. Nobody wants to work hard to understand a message. In the following rewritten version, notice how the list makes the steps easier to read and understand. Also note that it's numbered—because the steps need to be taken in a certain order—and that each item begins with a present-tense verb, so the list is parallel.

Our HR department has designed a program encouraging employees to use public transportation when going to and from work. Enrollment on the askhr.com site includes four steps:

1. Select the mass transit you'll be using.

2. Read the Commuter Reimbursement Plan (available on the company portal) and select your preferred method of reimbursement.

3. Sign up for the program, offered through AD Systems, and select which options are applicable.

4. Complete all three forms (mass transit options, reimbursement plan, and sign-up), and submit them through the company portal.

Decide if, and if so where, a list format might be an effective technique to use in your messages. Be careful though—don't over itemize, as that will make your writing read like a grocery list and, thus, lose its effectiveness.

Risks/Consequences

If your writing isn't easy to read and follow, readers can get lost, might become frustrated, and may not even read your message. Or they may skim it or skip parts and, consequently, not comprehend the complete or correct meaning. This kind of confusion can lead to costly mistakes with relatively simple messages, such as those addressing product orders or service schedules.

Likewise, if your writing could potentially have more than one meaning, the reader may misinterpret it, causing you to spend extra time straightening out misunderstandings through additional messages or conversations. And since your writing is a reflection of you, foggy writing hurts your credibility. In contrast, clear writing tells your customers and employees they can trust you—that you're a smart, clear thinker.

Would you want to do business with the writer who sends this foggy message?

It is our intention to make every effort to deliver your material by the date of June 8, which you requested.

Wait, what? What material? Wait, " . . . make every effort . . . "? How is the reader supposed to make an intelligent, informed business decision with that kind of message? So, no, you probably don't want to do business with them. What about doing business with a person who sends this message?

We will schedule a June 8 delivery of your order #62D777: 278 yards of patterned nylon fabric.

That's the writer with whom you want to do business!

Clear Scan

As the writer, it isn't enough that you know what you mean—your writing has to be easy to read and perfectly clear to its intended reader. You can't expect your audience to read your mind or use a decoder ring to figure out what you're trying to say.

Abby scans the message for this BACKBONE component: clarity. Specifically, she's looking to see if she uses appropriate words, writes in a fluent style, and employs document design techniques that make the message easy to read and understand.

Misaligned Message with Clear Diagnosis

TO: Chris Martinez
FROM: Abby Shultz
DATE: October 1, 2022
SUBJECT: RE: Request to Attend Conference

Hi Chris,

I appreciate your interest in attending the *We're Wired* IT conference—staying current in our industry is important to both your professional development and our department's goals. ☺ [*emojis don't look professional and could be misunderstood by the reader*]

In 2021, for professional development, because our department is budgeted for $10K, we encourage employees' continuing education. [*awkward because it doesn't make sense, making it difficult to understand*] Due to the high volume of applications and approvals since January, people have really been clambering [*not an everyday, conversational business word*] for the remaining $500 LOL. [*text speak is inappropriate in workplace email*] I'd be glad to discuss alternative ways to support your professional development for this year, such as attending the virtual option of the *We're Wired* conference, finding a local conference to attend, or securing the remaining conference costs from other sources, and I want to make sure we secure that $500 for you; so, let me know by October 5 if you'd like to meet to discuss your options. Other possible funding sources are listed in the HR Professional Development folder. [*paragraph is too long, addresses more than one idea, lacks fluency, and is difficult to read*]

Thanks for taking initiative regarding your continuing professional development.

Best,
Abby

Abby Shultz, PMP
Director of Operations
DK Solutions
444.555.4321 // Direct

Clear Adjustments

See how Abby improves the readability of this message with some clear adjustments.

Properly Aligned Message with Clear Adjustments

TO: Chris Martinez
FROM: Abby Shultz
DATE: October 1, 2022
SUBJECT: RE: Request to Attend Conference

Hi Chris,

I appreciate your interest in attending the *We're Wired* IT conference—staying current in our industry is important to both your professional development and our department's goals. [omits emoji]

Because we encourage employees' continuing education, our department budgeted $10K for professional development in 2022. [rewords sentence to be logical, clear, and coherent] However, [inserts "however," providing a smooth transition from one thought to the next] due to the high volume of applications and approvals since January, only $500 remains available. [deletes pompous word "clambering" and omits text speak "LOL"]

I'd be glad to discuss alternatives that would help you prepare for the software updates such as
- Attending the virtual option of the *We're Wired* conference
- Completing a vendor-provided online training program
- Securing the remaining conference costs from other sources, as listed in the HR Professional Development folder [divides information into several shorter paragraphs and uses bullet points to aid clarity]

I want to make sure we secure that $500 for you; so, let me know by October 5 if you'd like to meet to discuss your options. [separates idea into its own paragraph]

Thanks for taking initiative regarding your continuing professional development.

Best,
Abby

Abby Shultz, PMP
Director of Operations
DK Solutions
444.555.4321 // Direct

Notice how Abby's clear adjustments focus on precise and appropriate words, sentence fluency and variety, and design/format—making the message easy to read and understand.

If you've ever tried to drive in fog, you understand how nerve-racking it can be. So, make your messages clear for optimal visibility and easy navigation. Your readers' journey should be obstacle free so they can effortlessly cruise through your message and clearly see your meaning.

BACKBONE Adjustments: What to Check Before You Click "Send"

- Word Choice—appropriate for reader and context; conversational style
- Sentences—fewer than 20 words each
- Fluency—transitions incorporated; sentence structure varied
- Readability—easy to read and only one way to interpret
- Design Techniques—effective use of white space and graphic highlighting

Keen

Readers are often influenced by attributes of writing that aren't obvious. As a writer, you can look through your style microscope to identify and use important subtle strategies to influence your readers' reactions. To elicit a positive reaction from your readers, draw them in by employing techniques designed to boost engagement. This connection with your readers, along with precision and enthusiasm, makes your messages keen, giving them the edge they need to be sharp and focused.

Let's magnify and examine ways to give your writing a keen edge. After all, nobody wants to read dull email. Keen is the way to go.

Dull

I have time to review the regional quarterly sales numbers on 6/17 at 2:00. The principal focus will be on identifying marketing strategies for regional supervisors. I have decided that supervisors need assistance in reaching their new target goals.

Keen

To help you review your regional quarterly sales numbers, let's meet at 2:00 p.m. on Thursday, 6/17. The principal focus will be on identifying marketing strategies for your regional supervisors. Together, we can provide guidance for them as they work toward reaching their new target goals.

I look forward to working with you as we explore this new marketing initiative!

Like a well-cut diamond, a keen email is inviting—it makes your readers want to take a closer look. So, draw readers in by attending to the details that give a message that healthy, irresistible glow of being reader centered, enthusiastic, and sharp.

Strategies

1. Incorporate the "You" Attitude

In the bicentric chapter, we provided general strategies to analyze your audience; now, let's take a closer look at those readers for whom you've created a basic reader profile. Go beyond knowing, for example, how many readers there will be or how they might react to your message. Pay very close attention to honing some of the finer points of that general analysis.

The first key to this refinement is to apply a "you" attitude in your writing. In this case "you" means the reader. With this approach, you (the writer) anticipate the reader's wants and needs. Readers usually ask, "What's in it for me?" Use this knowledge to maximize the impact of your message: Stress the "you" attitude rather than the "me" attitude.

The "you" attitude emphasizes what readers want to know and how they'll be affected by the message; it requires developing empathy—the ability to project yourself into another person's position and to understand that person's situation, feelings, motives, and needs.

One important component of the "you" attitude is targeting reader benefits, emphasizing how the reader will benefit from doing as you ask—a powerful strategy in written communication.

Note the differences in the following messages, which both convey the same main idea:

"Me" Attitude:
We are happy to announce that we are offering commercial retail space on the corner of Hudson and Market. We will sell this space for $825,000. We originally purchased this unit to house our extension office, but our plans have changed.

"You" Attitude:
You now have the opportunity to purchase a commercial retail space on the corner of Hudson and Market for $825,000, ten percent below market value. The property is zoned C-2 for light commercial use, so you could expand your

current unit's square footage by 50 percent. We would be glad to give you a free analysis of how this space could benefit your existing business.

One difference between those two messages is pronoun use. The "you" attitude message employs more second person pronouns ("you"), which address the reader directly. "You now have the opportunity … ," "…you could expand…," and "…glad to give you…." The "me" attitude version contains no second person pronouns; it's too self-centered to foster an effective connection with the reader.

The other difference is that the "you" attitude version includes reader benefits—below-market-value price, zoning information, and possible expansion of square footage.

2. Avoid Discriminatory Language

Reader-centered messages always employ nondiscriminatory language. Bias-free language treats everyone equally, making no unwarranted assumptions about any person or group. Competent, keen communicators make sure their writing is free of sexist language and bias based on age, ability, ethnicity, race, religion, gender identification, and sexual orientation—all of which are protected by federal laws.

Look at this example from a poorly written incident report:

Two girls from the Fraud Unit accused a salesman of sexual harassment. Caroline Taylor, a data entry clerk, and Anne Bonini, a receptionist, accused David Lee of making suggestive comments. Lee, who is 57 years old and suffers from a psychiatric disorder, denied the charges.

This message contains unnecessary discriminatory language:

- Sexist language: *girls, salesman*
- Age: *57 years old*
- Disability: *suffers from a psychiatric disorder*

This version of the report is bias free:

A data entry clerk and a receptionist from the Fraud Unit filed a report accusing a sales associate of sexual harassment. The sales associate denied the charges.

To avoid sex bias in writing, do one of the following: 1) use plural nouns so that the subject can be referred to with the plural pronoun *they* or 2) reword the sentence to avoid pronouns. The second option, though, usually changes your writing to passive voice—which is fine to use once in a while.

Biased:

The supervisor must submit his timesheets to the HR manager every Friday by noon. (Assumes anyone who's a supervisor is male.)

Not Biased:

1. *Supervisors must submit their timesheets to the HR manager every Friday by noon.* (Makes both the subject and pronoun plural.)

2. *Supervisors' timesheets must be submitted to the HR manager every Friday by noon.* (Passive voice eliminates the need for a pronoun.)

If you follow trends in our ever-evolving language, you know you can now use the pronoun "they" to refer to either a singular or plural antecedent: *The supervisor must submit their timesheets to the HR manager every Friday by noon.*

Using nondiscriminatory language is a smart business practice because it's ethical, it reduces the risk of offending readers, and it protects you legally.

3. Develop an Enthusiastic Style

Enthusiastic writing conveys powerful energy; a lack of enthusiasm can cause a power outage. When conveying positivity and enthusiasm in person, you can control nonverbal factors in your voice such as volume, pitch, and pace. You also help others interpret your meaning through nonverbal cues such as facial expressions and gestures. So how can you control those nonverbal—not words—aspects of your writing so you convey enthusiasm? Easily: through word choice and punctuation.

Bland:
I think you did a good job on your report.

Enthusiastic:
John, your report was well organized, complete, and focused. Well done!

We bet John can feel the virtual pat on the back in the enthusiastic version. In version two, the sentence begins with the reader, rather than the writer, in mind. (The writer uses the reader's name rather than the pronoun "I.") More than generalizing with "good job," the enthusiastic version provides concrete details—"well organized, complete, and focused." And for added energy, the enthusiastic message ends with a compliment followed by an exclamation point—that's ONE exclamation point only . . . always just one. (And please don't put an exclamation point at the end of every sentence in an email; just like anything else, exclamation points lose their effectiveness if overused.)

4. Choose Precise, Concrete Words and Phrases

Concentrate on using precise, rather than vague, words so your message can be easily understood. For example, what exactly do you mean when writing that you'd like someone to "contact you soon"? Should they call? Write? Visit? In the next hour? This week? Next month? The more specific you are, the more likely readers will understand your message and respond as requested.

Which of the following signs is more likely to accomplish its purpose?

Dull:

Anyone caught parking a non-electric vehicle in this area will be dealt with accordingly.

Where, exactly, is "this area"? And what does "dealt with accordingly" mean? Fined? Fired?

Keen:

Anyone caught parking a non-electric vehicle within 20 feet of this charging station will be fined $500.

So now readers know exactly where they can't park their non-electric vehicles (within 20 feet of the charging station) and what will happen if they do (a $500 fine).

Use precise verbs:

Vague: *HR will give you a new parking pass.*

Precise: *HR will email you a new parking pass on March 1.*

Use specific nouns:

General: *We have many things to discuss in the next sales meeting.*

Specific: *We have three sales-improving strategies to discuss in the next meeting.*

5. Use the Correct Words

Set your writing apart by using correct words; don't fall prey to misusing commonly confused words.

Incorrect: *The members of the financial committee submitted there annual report.*

Correct: *The members of the financial committee submitted their annual report.*

Risks/Consequences

Email readers have expectations. They expect messages that are enthusiastic and sharp—keen. While your readers know the message is for them, that doesn't mean they'll feel important or be interested in what you have to say.

And even if your audience reads your less-than-keen message, they may feel alienated, apathetic, or bored. The more likely outcome, however, will be that they just close and forget about the message. You're not going to sell a lot of insurance policies—or accomplish whatever your purpose is—with communication that isn't keen. Email that's focused on—and written specifically for—a targeted audience is keen, effective email.

Keen Scan

Abby knows that a good start is to just type the first words that come to mind. But, to make sure she uses sharp, enthusiastic, nondiscriminatory language and incorporates the "you" attitude, she scans for keen-ness.

Misaligned Message with Keen Diagnosis

TO: Chris Martinez
FROM: Abby Shultz
DATE: October 1, 2022
SUBJECT: RE: Request to Attend Conference

Hi Chris,

I've heard of that [avoids "you" attitude] We're Wired conference that guys like to attend [shows sex bias]. Staying current in our industry is important to professional development and our department's goals.

Because we encourage employees' continuing education, our department budgeted some money [needs precise language] for professional development in 2022. However, do [uses a wrong word] to the high volume of applications and approvals since January, there is not much left [lacks specificity].

I'd be glad to discuss alternative ways to support professional development for this year such as
- Attending the virtual option of the We're Wired conference
- Finding a local conference to attend
- Securing the remaining conference costs from other sources listed in the HR Professional Development folder

It would be nice to secure the $500 [doesn't convey enthusiasm and "you" attitude]; so, let me know as soon as possible [vague phrasing] if you'd like to meet to discuss options.

Thanks for taking initiative regarding your continuing professional development.

Best,
Abby

Abby Shultz, PMP
Director of Operations
DK Solutions
444.555.4321 // Direct

Keen Adjustments

Observe Abby's keen adjustments, which demonstrate "you" attitude and nondiscriminatory, enthusiastic, sharp language.

Properly Aligned Message with Keen Adjustments

TO: Chris Martinez
FROM: Abby Shultz
DATE: October 1, 2022
SUBJECT: RE: Request to Attend Conference

Hi Chris,

I appreciate your interest in attending the *We're Wired* IT conference—staying current in our industry is important to both your professional development and our department's goals. *[demonstrates "you" attitude and avoids sexist language]*

Because we encourage employees' continuing education, our department budgeted $10K *[states specific amount]* for professional development in 2022. However, due *[uses correct word]* to the high volume of applications and approvals since January, only $500 *[states exact amount]* remains available.

I'd be glad to discuss alternatives *[conveys enthusiasm about finding a solution]* that would help you prepare for the software updates such as
* Attending the virtual option of the *We're Wired* conference
* Completing a vendor-provided online training program
* Securing the remaining conference costs from other sources listed in the <u>HR Professional Development</u> folder

I want to make sure we secure that $500 for you; so, let me know by October 5 *[suggests a specific date]* if you'd like to meet to discuss your options.

Thanks for taking initiative regarding your *[shows "you" attitude]* continuing professional development.

Best,
Abby

Abby Shultz, PMP
Director of Operations
DK Solutions
444.555.4321 // Direct

Abby's keen adjustments demonstrate her communication charisma by incorporating "you" attitude and sharp language. Skilled email writers know their readers and adapt their messages to facilitate effective communication. Demonstrate your communication moxie by making sure your writing is keen.

BACKBONE Adjustments: What to Check Before You Click "Send"
• "You" Attitude—considers reader's needs and wants; includes reader benefits
• Nondiscriminatory Language—free of sexist and biased language
• Enthusiastic Style—conveys energy
• Word Choice—precise, concrete, and correct

Buff

Imagine an email message as a buff Olympic gymnastics champion: it arrives in your inbox as a commanding presence. As a power-packed message, it contains only relevant information conveyed clearly and concisely—an economy of motion. No fat. Just a strong, lean message that starts with a pop, moves skillfully in a logical direction, and ends with a solid action statement. At the conclusion of the message, readers know exactly what they need to do.

Like a buff athlete, buff writing is trim and muscular. It communicates a fit, robust message without any flabby components such as irrelevant information, unnecessary repetition, abstract or pompous language, or words just along for the ride.

Strategies

Trim sentences are like trim bodies—they take work. The following strategies can help optimize the muscle mass of your written communication, making sure it's buff rather than flabby.

1. Use a Conversational Style

Use simple, conversational language rather than try to sound super smart (even though you are). Pompous, convoluted language is not an indicator of intelligence or competent communication abilities—don't succumb to the temptation! For a solid first draft email, just write the way you'd speak in that workplace situation, to that particular audience—be professionally conversational.

Flabby:
Illumination is required to be extinguished on these premises upon cessation of daily activities.

Buff:
Turn off the lights when you leave the building.

Here, the buff example eliminates the euphemisms (such as "illumination" for "lights") and reshapes the pompous-sounding construction of "is required to be extinguished" to read "turn off."

There's no need to be fancy. Write the way you'd talk to that person in that context.

2. Include Relevant Information Only

How do you determine what content to include in a message? Consider the two driving factors: purpose and audience. Then write what needs to be conveyed for readers to understand the information and take action. Make decisions about what content to include based on the readers' perspective.

If you need to send, for example, a "save the date and time" message to remote employees informing them of an upcoming virtual all-hands meeting, stick to that information only. Don't include superfluous content that might distract them from the main idea.

Flabby:
Please save a one-hour spot in your calendar for a virtual all-hands meeting that will be held on Monday, July 20 at 11:00 a.m. CST. The actual meeting invitation will be sent out via email later this week. Just accept that invitation, and the link to the meeting will show up in your calendar.

Buff:
Later this week you'll receive an Outlook invitation to the all-hands meeting scheduled for 11:00 a.m. CST on Monday, July 20.

Due to the information revolution, people have easy access to a lot of data. Having more information to analyze (and no extra time), readers want information presented concisely.

3. Ensure Every Word Adds Value

Flabby:

It is perfectly clear that phone calls held on a weekly basis are the most effective kind of calls.

Buff:

Weekly phone calls are most effective.

In this example, the flabby version starts with the impersonal pronoun "it," and the reader doesn't know what "it" is until the end of the sentence. And even then, it's still not very clear. Generally, avoid starting a sentence with zombie phrases such as *It is/are/were, Here is/are,* and *There is/are/were.* Also, the prepositional phrase "on a weekly basis" is unnecessary since "weekly" will do. Imagine that— one word substituting for four.

The leaner, buff version starts with the subject "weekly phone calls" and moves directly to answering the question, "What about the weekly phone calls?" This puts what's important at the front of the sentence, making the sentence's point easy to find.

Flabby:

Although the shrinkage rates for the third quarter are high in number, experience has indicated that it is not an unusual condition for the Chicago market.

Buff:

Third quarter high shrinkage rates are normal for the Chicago market.

The buff version trims the fat by eliminating wordy expressions and redundancies such as the double negative "not an unusual," the meaningless "experience has indicated that," the unnecessary "in number," and the prepositional phrase "for the third quarter." This results in a lean, concise sentence—muscular and trim. Challenge yourself to convey your point concisely.

4. Default to Active Voice

One of the easiest ways to make your writing trim and muscular is to write in active voice rather than passive voice.

Passive:

The dogs of the employees may be brought to work by employees only on the day designated as Bring Your Dog to Work Day.

Active:

Employees may bring their dogs to work only on Bring Your Dog to Work Day.

You can see that the active voice sentence is shorter—15 words rather than 24. What accounts for that difference?

- The subject "Employees" is now at the beginning of the sentence.
- The verb phrase "may be brought" is shortened to "may bring."
- Four prepositional phrases have been eliminated: "of the employees," "into work," "by employees," and "on the day."

Active voice is writing muscle. The active voice (*I did it*) displays more accountability and is more direct and concise than the passive voice (*It was done by me*). Some writers rely on passive voice because they think it sounds more objective, important, or sophisticated. But passive voice makes writing wordy and gives the impression the writer may be hesitant, indecisive, or evasive. Consider the effect when a passive statement is recast in the active voice:

Passive voice—wordy and indirect:
Labor costs for this project were underestimated by me.

Passive voice—evasive:
Labor costs for this project were underestimated.

Active voice—concise and direct (use this one—own your actions):
I underestimated labor costs for this project.

Active voice is economical, direct, and clear. Approximately 80 percent of your sentences should be in active voice. Be careful though—make sure to vary your sentences so they're not all in subject-verb-object construction. Readers need variety in order to stay engaged; plus, there may be times when you want, or need, to use passive voice. When?

- When you don't know the subject (the do-er of the action—in this case who parked the car): *A red Kia Sorento has been parked in the new landscaping area.*

- If the subject is not important: *The announcement about the new director of finance will be emailed today.*

- If you want to avoid placing blame: *A coffee maker in the 2nd floor break room was left on overnight, overheated, and now must be replaced.*

- When you want to create suspense: *This month's employee raffle prize has been won by Rick Gibson.*

As you can see, buff sentences are muscular and trim. They're shorter, easier to read, contain no excess information, and usually begin with their subject. They take less time to write and promote well-informed, quick, easy responses—all factors that save time and money.

Risks/Consequences

The major consequences of flabby workplace emails are lack of impact and lack of efficiency. In order to make the desired impact, your message must be read by the audience. And to be efficient, readers must understand your meaning easily.

If readers can't read your message quickly, they may not read it at all. In that case, the chances of accomplishing your purpose are significantly reduced. If readers are confused by or misunderstand your message, or if your communication path is riddled with wads of words and punctuation litter, your audience may not make the effort to decipher your message.

Buff Scan

Knowing strong emails have a low percentage of communication fat, Abby scans her draft message for conciseness, active voice, and information relevancy.

Misaligned Message with Buff Diagnosis

TO: Chris Martinez
FROM: Abby Shultz
DATE: October 1, 2022
SUBJECT: RE: Request to Attend Conference

Hi Chris,

Your interest in attending the *We're Wired* IT conference is appreciated by me—staying current in our industry is important to both your professional development and our department's goals. *[passive voice is wordy and awkward]*

Because we encourage all employees' continuing education efforts, our department has budgeted $10K for professional development for calendar year 2022. However, due to the high volume of applications and approvals since January, only $500 dollars remains available to be used. *[nine unnecessary words make the paragraph verbose]*

I'd be glad to discuss alternative ways to support your professional development for this year such as
- Attending the virtual option of the *We're Wired* conference
- Finding a local conference to attend
- Securing the remaining conference costs from other sources listed in the <u>HR Professional Developmen</u> folder, created in 2018. *[irrelevant information]*

I want to make sure we secure that $500 for you; so, let me know by October 5 if you'd like to meet to discuss your options.

Thanks for taking initiative regarding your continuing professional development.

Best,
Abby

Abby Shultz, PMP
Director of Operations
DK Solutions
444.555.4321 // Direct

Buff Adjustments

Notice how Abby's Buff adjustments make the message stronger and leaner—more concise.

Properly Aligned Message with Buff Adjustments

TO: Chris Martinez
FROM: Abby Shultz
DATE: October 1, 2022
SUBJECT: RE: Request to Attend Conference

Hi Chris,

I appreciate your interest in attending the *We're Wired* IT conference—staying current in our industry is important to both your professional development and our department's goals. *[active voice is concise]*

Because we encourage employees' continuing education, our department budgeted $10K for professional development in 2022. However, due to the high volume of applications and approvals since January, only $500 remains available. *[lean text makes this paragraph 31 words rather than 40—nearly 25 percent shorter]*

I'd be glad to discuss alternatives that would help you prepare for the software updates such as
- Attending the virtual option of the *We're Wired* conference
- Completing a vendor-provided online training program
- Securing the remaining conference costs from other sources listed in the HR Professional Development folder *[irrelevant information about when the folder was created is eliminated]*

I want to make sure we secure that $500 for you; so, let me know by October 5 if you'd like to meet to discuss your options.

Thanks for taking initiative regarding your continuing professional development.

Best,
Abby

Abby Shultz, PMP
Director of Operations
DK Solutions
444.555.4321 // Direct

Abby's adjustments reduce the number of words and eliminate unnecessary information, making the message buff.

Since buff writing is muscular and easy to read, it saves readers time and reduces misunderstandings that could lead to uninformed decisions or costly mistakes. Buff writing is strong, trim, and lean. Remember what Zorro taught his son: "Get in, make your 'Z,' and get out!" Now that's buff!

BACKBONE Adjustments: What to Check Before You Click "Send"

• Relevant Information—unnecessary information removed
• Conversational Style—as you'd speak to that audience, in that situation
• Conciseness—only words that add value are included
• Active Voice—80 percent of sentences (subject does the action on the verb)

Ordered

Ordered

Also critical to your communication success is making sure your messages are well organized. We all know people who are good at telling jokes; likewise, we all know people who aren't such good joke tellers. One difference between these two groups is the ability to organize information in a logical, coherent fashion.

> Poor joke teller: A bartender says, "We don't serve food." A sandwich walks into a bar and orders a beer. [Silence.]
> Good joke teller: A sandwich walks into a bar and orders a beer. The bartender says, "We don't serve food." [Rim shot.]

A great joke teller puts joke content in a logical order, presenting the punch line in just the right place for a laugh. A poor joke teller may give the punchline too early or skip information necessary to understand the intended humor—no wonder nobody laughs. Jokes don't make sense when the information isn't in a logical, coherent order.

Similarly, in writing emails, the order of the information matters. Ordering your message appropriately can make the difference between success and failure in getting your ideas across. So remember, when you communicate, you can't just toss an unorganized pile of ideas on readers and expect them to figure out what you mean; they shouldn't have to complete a lexical jigsaw puzzle to see the point of the message. Instead, give them an ordered whole—a structured message with information presented in a logical order.

Strategies

1. Plan Your Message

Just as good joke tellers have the joke's storyline in mind before they start delivering the joke, you should create some kind of outline before writing your email. Do it in your head, with voice notes, in a document, on a cocktail napkin—whatever. You don't need anything formal, so use any method you like. An outline is a good tool to help you organize your information—to get your storyline in your head before you write. Don't be that person who thinks as long as all the information is there, that's good enough. Outlines force you to think before you write, which is the only way to make sure your message is organized.

You may think creating an outline adds precious time to the writing process. But ultimately, outlining saves time. First, it's an easy way to get started on your message right away. Second, the actual time spent writing your email will be reduced because you've spent time preparing it—you've already thought about what you want to say (purpose) to that particular reader (audience) and how the content should be organized (order). Third, because you planned, you'll spend less time revising the message. Also, you won't need to clean up any messes caused by readers misunderstanding a message conveyed via a babbling stream of consciousness.

2. Structure Your Message

Well-ordered messages have structure. To be clearly understood and easily followed, information in a message must have a beginning, middle, and end.

Beginning
Subject Line
Greeting
First Sentence

Middle
Paragraphs
Lists

End
Friendly Ending
Sign-off

Beginning

Subject Line: Although not included in the message itself, your subject line introduces your email. It makes an impression and determines whether or not your email gets noticed, opened, read, and easily retrieved. An effective subject line has two parts: 1) signal words that tell the purpose and 2) a do/know statement that indicates the specific topic related to the purpose. For example,

Subject: *Invitation to Company Picnic*

The signal words "Invitation to" signify that the email's purpose is to invite readers. The do/know statement "Company Picnic" tells readers to what they're being invited.

Following are other sample signal words and do/know statements:

Signal Words
Request for
Information about
Proposal to

Do/Know Statement
Paid Time Off
Flexible Healthcare Spending
Advertising Budget Increase

Greeting: Think about the reader and your relationship with that person before you write the greeting. For example, are you on a first-name basis? If not, find out how the reader prefers to be addressed and use that as the greeting. And, of course, make sure you spell their name correctly.

Greetings to Avoid
To Whom It May Concern:
Dear Sir or Madam:
Hey peeps,

Informal Greetings
Hi,
Hi John,
Hi everyone—

Formal Greetings
Mr. Brown,
Dear Dr. Lopez:
Hello Ms. Smith:

NOTE: Using a colon rather than a comma after the greeting is considered very formal for email messages. Using "To Whom It May Concern" or "Dear Sir or Madam" is lazy; find out the person's name or position and use it.

First Sentence: The goal of your email's first sentence is to connect with the reader before jumping into the topic.

Avoid
Getting immediately to the point
My name is Anne and I'm a . . .
The purpose of this email is . . .

Start on a Positive Note
Common bond or connection: *I read your recent article on [whatever] in [some publication].*
Compliment: *I'm glad we're working together again.*
Thank you: *Thank you for your help gathering the evaluation scores.*

NOTE: Make sure the first sentence is sincere and relates to the information discussed in the email. For example, don't say, "I hope you're experiencing nice weather" if your message isn't about the weather.

Middle

In the Clear chapter, we mentioned keeping paragraphs short (fewer than seven lines). But you also want to limit the number of paragraphs in an email to approximately three to five. It's an email, not a novel. If you need more than five paragraphs to complete your message, put the information in an attachment.

End

Friendly Ending: Finding the right tone to close emails requires thought and finesse. Avoid clichés, such as *Thank you for your time and consideration*, as well as negatively stated endings, such as *Please do not hesitate to call me.* Three good examples of friendly endings are

> *Thanks for your help with the financial analysis.*
> *Great working with you on the Spencer Project!*
> *Please let me know if you have any questions about the Flextime Initiative.*

Sign-off: Without a professional sign-off, your email message may seem to end too abruptly, or you may come across as someone who doesn't care about professional niceties or nuances. Use a sign-off that's genuine to your personality and tailored to your relationship with the reader.

Too Informal: *Later, XOXO, Ciao, Thx,*
Less Formal: *Cheers, Thanks, Warmly, Talk soon,*
Formal: *Best/Best wishes, Kind/Best regards, Thank you, With appreciation,*
Very Formal or Outdated: *Yours truly, Regards, Sincerely yours, Cordially,*

Overall, when in doubt, err on the side of being slightly too formal.

Signature: Use your first name only or first and last name depending on the formality of your message and your relationship with the reader. If your organization has a prescribed email signature block, be sure to use it. If not, design your own signature block to include name, title, company, email address, phone number, and any other pertinent contact information. Avoid using quotes as part of your signature block, and don't use wallpaper in workplace email. Also, you may want a separate email signature for Reply messages.

3. Select an Appropriate Organizational Pattern

Various messages require different patterns of organization (e.g., direct or indirect) depending on the purpose and anticipated reader reaction.

Use direct organization for good/positive news, neutral news, goodwill messages, and, in some situations, persuasive messages:

1. Start with a positive note
2. State the main message
3. Provide background information
4. Include an action statement, if applicable
5. Close with a friendly ending

Use indirect organization for most bad news, messages that may be taken negatively, and, in some situations, persuasive messages:

1. Start with a positive note
2. Provide background information
3. State the main message
4. Provide a counterproposal
5. Include an action statement, if applicable
6. Close with a friendly ending

After you've established your purpose and considered your audience's potential reactions, you'll know whether to organize your message in a direct or indirect pattern.

You might be tempted to just start writing without making a plan, but you know better (see Strategy #1): there may be consequences associated with short cuts, all of which will cost you time and could hurt your credibility.

Let's say your employees were looking forward to enjoying the flexibility of a four-day work week, and your executive committee agreed to make it an option. If you don't organize the information before you communicate this good news to employees, your message might ramble and jump around, as the following example illustrates:

On July 16, the executive committee met at Blacklick Retreat in Sausalito. All but one member attended. Martin Brown from Upbeat, Inc. presented an analysis of research on productivity. Mr. Brown has visited all of our departments during the last three months, speaking to mid-level managers and some of their employees. This allowed him to gather data about our daily production, employee attendance records, and overhead costs. The executive committee unanimously agreed with his recommendation that we adopt an optional four-day work week for all employees, starting August 1. To sign up, employees must complete the Flexible Work Schedule form on the company's website by July 25. Mr. Brown's presentation included a description of the effectiveness of a variety of work schedules. His recommendation was that flexible schedules increase productivity and morale and reduce absenteeism and turnover.

Initially, readers may not have read the message due to its length. And if they did start reading it, they may have quit because of poor organization (for example, the main idea, which is positive, is buried in the middle). Since this message is good news for most readers, it should follow the direct pattern of organization, with the main idea at or near the beginning.

Taking time to create a basic plan or outline, and using it to organize the message, results in a much better message than the verbal diarrhea in the preceding email.

1. **Positive note:** The executive committee recently approved an exciting flextime opportunity for employees.

2. **Main message:** On August 1, the company will offer an optional four-day work week.

3. **Background information:** When, where, who attended, and Mr. Brown's research, presentation, and recommendation.

4. **Action statement:** To sign up, employees must complete the Flexible Work Schedule form on the company's website before July 25.

5. **Friendly ending:** We're excited to offer you flextime options as a benefit of your employment.

Start with that information, in that order, and draft your message.

But what about messages that communicate negative information? Let's say the executive committee decided not to offer an optional four-day work week. This is going to be bad news for many employees.

As shown previously, jot down a list or make an informal outline of the point you want to address in your message. But since it's bad news, use the indirect pattern of organization.

1. **Positive note:** Thank executive committee for researching a four-day work week flextime option.

2. **Background information:** Include research on four-day work week productivity, evidence, coverage, and scheduling concerns.

3. **Main message:** Four-day work week won't be an option.

4. **Counterproposal:** The committee will consider other flextime options at its next meeting in December.

5. **Action statement:** Take this opportunity to submit suggestions (by October 1) for flextime program hours that consider daily coverage needs for your department.

6. **Positive ending:** We look forward to working with you as we continue to examine your flextime options.

Remember that messages require different patterns of organization depending on their purpose and anticipated reader reactions. Within these organizational patterns, make sure your information is logically presented—chronological, cause/effect, topical, etc.—and you've included transitional words and phrases such as *next, however, furthermore, alternatively*, etc.

Overall, good organization reduces the time and energy readers need to

- Understand the message because there's a logical, coherent flow that aids comprehension

- Accept the message because they believe your reasoning/thinking is sound, just like your message's organization

- Take appropriate action because they know what needs to be done and what step to take first

Risks/Consequences

A poorly organized message could obscure important information, causing readers to overlook vital facts, become confused, or make poor decisions. Or readers could be so perplexed or bored they stop reading—not the result you want!

Poor organization also could cause readers to form a negative impression of you. While readers may think you're competent, a poorly organized message may lead them to believe you're not a clear thinker or communicator. Or worse, they may think you don't care much about them—that they weren't worth your time to organize the message clearly. Again, not the result you want!

Ordered Scan

Abby knows she can't expect readers to figure out a jumbled mess. So, for this scan, she's making sure all of the parts are there and in a logical order.

Misaligned Message with Ordered Diagnosis

TO: Chris Martinez
FROM: Abby Shultz
DATE: October 1, 2022
SUBJECT: Conference *[subject line doesn't contain signal words and a do/know statement]*

[missing a greeting and a positive note for the first sentence]
Due to the high volume of applications and approvals since January, only $500 remains for professional development. Because we encourage employees' continuing education, our department budgeted $10K for professional development in 2022. *[ineffective organizational pattern: using the direct arrangement for negative messages is abrupt and reduces the reader's acceptance of the message]*

I'd be glad to discuss alternative ways to support your professional development for this year such as
- Attending the virtual option of the *We're Wired* conference
- Finding a local conference to attend
- Securing the remaining conference costs from other sources listed in the <u>HR Professional Development</u> folder

I want to make sure we secure that $500 for you; so, let me know by October 5 if you'd like to meet to discuss your options.

[missing a friendly ending]

Best,
Abby

Abby Shultz, PMP
Director of Operations
DK Solutions
444.555.4321 // Direct

Ordered Adjustments

Observe how Abby's ordered adjustments make her message easier to follow and understand.

Properly Aligned Message with Ordered Adjustments

TO: Chris Martinez
FROM: Abby Shultz
DATE: October 1, 2022
SUBJECT: RE: Request to Attend Conference
[subject line includes signal words (Request to) and a do/know statement (Attend Conference), clearly indicating what the message is about]

Hi Chris, *[greeting makes the message structured and professional]*

I appreciate your interest in attending the *We're Wired* IT conference—staying current in our industry is important to both your professional development and our department's goals. *[sincere, positive statement related to the message creates appropriate tone and buffers the negative news]*

Because we encourage employees' continuing education, our department budgeted $10K for professional development in 2022. However, due to the high volume of applications and approvals since January, only $500 remains available.

I'd be glad to discuss alternatives that would help you prepare for the software updates such as
- Attending the virtual option of the *We're Wired* conference
- Completing a vendor-provided online training program
- Securing the remaining conference costs from other sources listed in the <u>HR Professional Development</u> folder

I want to make sure we secure that $500 for you; so, let me know by October 5 if you'd like to meet to discuss your options. *[information organized to follow an indirect pattern for this bad news: positive note, background information, main message, counterproposal, action statement, and friendly ending]*

Thanks for taking initiative regarding your continuing professional development. *[friendly ending included]*

Best,
Abby

Abby Shultz, PMP
Director of Operations
DK Solutions
444.555.4321 // Direct

Notice how the indirect pattern of organization places the bad news in a position that makes the reader more likely to accept it. Plus, it looks more professional because Abby included all the basic parts of an email.

Just like you want people to "get" your jokes, you want readers to "get" your messages. For that to happen, organize your emails to be logical and uncluttered, with their purpose easy to locate and act on. To promote your clear, logical thinking and to increase the chance your message will be accepted (or at least get a fair reading), take time to organize the information you want to communicate.

BACKBONE Adjustments: What to Check Before You Click "Send"

Beginning:
- Subject Line—signal words and do-know statement
- Greeting—appropriate level of formality
- First Sentence—positive note that is sincere and related to the message

Middle:
- Length—maximum of five short paragraphs
- Information—presented in a logical order
- Appropriate Organizational Pattern—direct or indirect

End:
- Friendly Ending—genuine and tailored to the message
- Sign-off—appropriate level of formality
- Signature—appropriate for message formality and relationship with reader

Nourished

Nourished

Envision the fresh fruits and vegetables department in your favorite market; those colorful, natural products are full of nutrients your body needs to function properly and fight disease. When you eat well, the vitamins and minerals you consume nourish your body, giving you shiny hair, glowing skin, and energy to function productively.

Like your body, your emails also require nourishment. Each message you send should be complete—fortified with all the relevant information necessary to prevent the need for additional messages. There's nothing worse than an endless cycle of emails full of ambiguity or missing information that requires clarification.

Nourished messages include all essential communication micronutrients, saving time and eliminating frustration for both readers and writers. Complete messages also enhance your reputation and promote goodwill; readers appreciate knowing exactly what you're asking for or what you're offering to do. Plus, well-supplemented messages support efficient decision making because readers are readily equipped with the crucial information they need in order to take action.

So just like you nourish yourself for long-term health and productivity, learn to fortify your emails with all of the details and examples readers need.

And make sure messages are supplemented, if applicable, with relevant attachments, hyperlinks, or any other references readers need to clearly understand the message.

Strategies

1. Include All Essential Information

A message should give readers all the information they need to understand the main idea and make decisions. Nourished writing includes relevant and appropriate information suited to the readers and states where to find additional details and resources addressing questions they may have. The amount and type of information that make a message complete vary based on purpose and audience.

For example, you might write this email and think it's ready to send:
Our marketing meeting is Thursday from 1:00 to 2:00 p.m.

That message would be considered complete and ready to send if it's about a regular, recurring meeting. But if that's not the case, the message doesn't contain enough information—it's malnourished. To prevent readers from having to ask for clarification, nourish the message by providing answers to questions about the meeting such as:

- What's the purpose?
- Who should attend?
- What's the date?
- Where's it being held?
- How will the reader benefit?
- What's the reader's action item?

For example:
The next marketing meeting will be held on Thursday, March 14 from 1-2 p.m. in conference room 265. Kate Brown will present the new social media marketing strategy to be rolled out during the third quarter. You'll be trained on the requirements for using social media and have an opportunity to ask questions about potential impacts to your department. Please confirm your attendance before February 10 by clicking on the "REGISTER" link below.

Yes, we know the second message is longer than the first example. And, yes, you want your writing to be concise. But never sacrifice completeness for conciseness. In other words, don't leave out important information because you're trying to keep the message short.

2. Respond to Every Part of a Multi-question Email

If you receive a multi-question email, copy and paste the questions from the sender's original email and insert them into your reply. When writers don't address all issues in one message, a lot of time is wasted with back-and-forth messages. FRUSTRATING!

3. Incorporate Attachments and Hyperlinks (if Applicable)

Often, readers want or need information in addition to what's included in the body of an email. As you anticipate this need, decide what information would be better suited as an attachment or as a link to a shared storage system like Dropbox, OneDrive, Google Drive, Box, or SharePoint.

Sending links to supplemental materials rather than attaching them provides several advantages: no file size limits, improved security features, no delivery failure, added confidentiality, no downloading requirements, improved collaboration, etc.

Risks/Consequences

Incomplete messages hurt companies, often resulting in lost time, money, and business. All of the back and forth caused by incomplete messages can result in inconsistencies or mistakes, requiring time to make corrections and repair damage. Additionally, malnourished messages can result in even more serious consequences. For example, if an employee forgets to include lodging costs in an email discussing a conference proposal, then their company might have to absorb the cost of lodging participants, which could be thousands of dollars. Unfortunately, this type of error could also cost the employee their job.

Nourished Scan

Abby knows she needs to give readers all the information they require in order to accomplish her purpose and meet their needs. So, for this scan, she checks to make sure all essential information is included.

Misaligned Message with Nourished Diagnosis

TO: Chris Martinez
FROM: Abby Shultz
DATE: October 1, 2022
SUBJECT: RE: Request to Attend Conference

Hi Chris,

I appreciate your interest in attending the *We're Wired* IT conference—staying current in our industry is important to both your professional development and our department's goals.

Because we encourage employees' continuing education, our department budgeted for professional development in 2022. [How much money was budgeted?] Only $500 remains available. [Why is there only $500 left?]

I'd be glad to discuss alternative ways to support your professional development for this year. [What are some of the alternatives?]

I want to make sure we secure that $500 for you; so, let me know if you'd like to meet to discuss your options. [By when? Today? Tomorrow? Next week?] Other possible funding sources are listed in the HR Professional Development folder. [Where is this folder?]

Thanks for taking initiative regarding your continuing professional development.

Best,

Abby

Abby Shultz, PMP
Director of Operations
DK Solutions
444.555.4321 // Direct

Nourished Adjustments

Notice how Abby supplements the message so that she answers questions the reader might have.

Properly Aligned Message with Nourished Adjustments

TO: Chris Martinez
FROM: Abby Shultz
DATE: October 1, 2022
SUBJECT: RE: Request to Attend Conference

Hi Chris,

I appreciate your interest in attending the *We're Wired* IT conference—staying current in our industry is important to both your professional development and our department's goals.

Because we encourage employees' continuing education, our department budgeted $10K for professional development in 2022. [states how much money was budgeted] However, due to the high volume of applications and approvals since January, only $500 remains available. [explains why only $500 is available]

I'd be glad to discuss alternatives that would help you prepare for the software updates such as [lists possible alternatives]
- Attending the virtual option of the *We're Wired* conference
- Completing a vendor-provided online training program
- Securing the remaining conference costs from other sources listed in the HR Professional Development folder [provides a link to the folder]

I want to make sure we secure that $500 for you; so, let me know by October 5 if you'd like to meet to discuss your options. [specifies by what date Chris must respond]

Thanks for taking initiative regarding your continuing professional development.

Best,
Abby

Abby Shultz, PMP
Director of Operations
DK Solutions
444.555.4321 // Direct

Because Abby anticipates the reader's questions, she provides essential information that makes the message complete. These details reduce the need for a flurry of back-and-forth messages to clarify information that isn't included.

A nourished message, like a nourished body, is fortified with everything needed to support wholesome business communication. Think of a nourished message as having the informational vitamins, minerals, and essential oils needed to effectively combat the obnoxious free radicals of incomplete information and, thus, rock a healthy communication glow.

BACKBONE Adjustments: What to Check Before You Click "Send"
- Complete—all necessary information included
- Supplemented (if applicable)—visuals, hyperlinks, attachments

Error Free

Error Free

Sure, we live in a world where we accidentally order too much guacamole on a fast-food app, make a mistake entering information into a data field on a website, or enter an email address incorrectly. And, sometimes, we send emails containing embarrassing or distracting mistakes. Ever write "not" instead of "now"? We get it. Nobody's perfect—we all occasionally make a mistake. And although there may not be much we can do about fat thumb syndrome, there are ways to significantly reduce the number of errors in our email messages.

Let's start with standards, otherwise known as conventions. Picture yourself traveling abroad and needing to plug in your computer. But your plug won't fit into the outlet; the standards for the electrical socket wherever you are aren't the same as those in the United States. You spend valuable time trying to find an adaptor. Not knowing the local standards, or conventions, for the electrical outlets causes you to waste time finding a solution. Similarly, written communication also has conventions such as spelling, grammar, capitalization, punctuation, number usage, etc. Know, and correctly use, those conventions— don't make people go through a foreign-electrical-outlet kind of hassle in order to read your email.

Where email is concerned, neither "standards" nor "conventions" is a dirty word. (Trust us, we would know.) Conventions are the norms agreed on by professional and academic associations that monitor language usage and evolution. These conventions are important to workplace email because they provide guidelines for a professional communication code of conduct. Rules for the communication game make it easier for everyone to understand each other.

So why, then, do people make so many convention errors in their emails? Sometimes they haven't yet learned, or even been introduced to, standard business English conventions. Sometimes they're under time constraints—they hurry and get careless. Sometimes conventions have changed or evolved, as language does. And sometimes, sadly, people just don't care or don't think following conventions is important.

You may think people don't mind if your writing contains a few punctuation, spelling, or grammar errors. Actually, they do. And so should you. You're judged by your writing. Your email messages are an extension of you. Readers may not commend you on your strong written communication skills, but they certainly will notice if you write "their" instead of "there" or "your" rather than "you're." To most people, reading an email containing convention errors is like hearing a sharp knife scraping against a glass bottle. Don't subject your readers to such an unpleasant sensation.

Basically, error-free writing refers to 1) correct use of standard English conventions and 2) accuracy of the message's content. Strive for error-free emails by applying the following strategies.

Strategies

1. Eliminate Distractions

Put down the cheese puffs and switch to your "concentrating" music—whatever you need to do so you can focus on editing and proofreading.

2. Fine-Tune Your Grammar Skills

Elevate your English conventions skills to peak performance shape. Master the standards of English conventions by finding a training resource suited to your specific grammar fitness needs. Many good, free, interactive resources are available online. And since it's difficult to know and remember all the conventions, keep an up-to-date e-handbook or app handy for quick reference.

3. Check for Content Accuracy

Make sure what you write is factually correct—double check the accuracy of your information, including names (and how they're spelled), dates, and numbers. And check the "To" field to make sure you're sending your message to the right people. An auto-populating "To" field can unnecessarily complicate your life, so make sure you're the boss of it. Check that all links work and all attachments are *actually* attached. As legendary Wild West sharp shooting Wyatt Earp once said, "Fast is fine, but accuracy is everything." We hear you, Wyatt.

4. Keep it Clean

Error-free writing means you've minimized or, ideally, **eliminated** mistakes by reviewing your messages for typos, extra spaces, and spelling errors. This is time well spent.

Error-free writing also means you've correctly used the standards of the English language: grammar, punctuation, number usage, etc. Consult your e-handbook or app (see, we told you you'd need it) or your company's style guide. Don't think there is one? Ask around.

Small details make a difference. The following examples show how poor grammar or carelessness could impact both the reader's understanding of a message and impression of the writer or organization.

Email sent to supervisor:

> *I had a family emergency and had to leave out of town. I'm not sure if I can make it to the meeting tommarrow. If I am unable to make it I am forwarding you my sales report. I would really appreciated if you would review with the group. Plz replay back asap.*

Would this employee be on your list for a promotion?

Job posting on a fast-food restaurant sign:

> *Wanted: Losers*
>
> *Apply Within*

You'd think they'd want winners (or "closers") rather than losers operating their fryers of boiling grease!

Waterloo West High School in Iowa printed hundreds of diplomas as:

> *Waterlook West High School*

Would you want your high school misspelled on your diploma?

Direct Air's website splashed this across its homepage:

Veiw Our Destinations

We wouldn't go anywhere on an airline that can't spell "view"! Spoiler alert—it's no longer in business.

Let's not mince words: the writers responsible for the examples above look illiterate or careless at the very least. In workplace writing, a lack of skill or a lackadaisical attitude can be detrimental to your career, hurt your company's reputation, and cost you time and money. Take control—it's up to you to make sure your professional email is spotless **before** you send it.

5. Use Technology Wisely

Use spelling and grammar checkers with caution. Can the employee who sends an email referencing a fiscal report to stockholders be taken seriously if writing "fecal responsibility" throughout the entire email? Sorry, but nobody's spellchecker will catch that type of error. And look out for that auto correct—it's a sneaky SOB.

Also, watch for words that are spelled correctly but are actually the wrong word. For example, spell checkers won't catch often-confused words: *affect/ effect, principal/principle, it's/its, hear/here*, etc.

And take note of your muscle memory. Sometimes your fingers anticipate what your brain wants them to write and automatically type "your" when you just wanted to write "you." Learn what your idiosyncratic mistakes are and look for them in **every single message** you write.

So, while you should use technology, we implore you to use it productively— use spelling and grammar checkers, but don't rely on them exclusively. Remember, **you** are responsible for the final product. NEVER EVER rely solely on those tools to find all your mistakes.

6. Give Yourself Time to Edit and Proofread

We understand it's difficult to write emails that are error free. It's like staying in shape—seems fairly straightforward, but if it were, we'd all be super fit all the time. Like staying in shape, eliminating errors in your email takes time and effort; however, it will get easier and take less time the more you practice.

Editing, usually done after you complete your message, involves making sure your spelling, grammar, and punctuation meet the conventions for American business English. Proofreading is the last step to take before sending a message. It's your last chance to find and fix mistakes such as typos, missing or repeated words, extra spaces, etc.

Editing and proofreading are both important to sending error-free emails. And if you follow the advice in the previous chapters, you should end up with a message that's pretty much ready to go by the time you proofread it. Nonetheless, use one of these proofreading strategies before you click "Send":

- Read your messages slowly, out loud. When it comes to proofreading, this is probably the simplest and most valuable advice we can offer. You'll be amazed how many errors you'll catch. With 200+ emails in your inbox demanding your attention, it's easy to quickly type a reply and hit "Send." You'll want to do this, **but don't**. Read every message slowly, out loud before you click "Send."

- Make time for a cooling off period. It's important to pause before you click "Send." For shorter routine messages, take your hands off the keyboard for a minute—it's not a steering wheel—and take a breath. For a more complex and longer email, write the message and save it as a draft so you can go back and review it later—an hour or a day—whatever time frame works. A cooling off period gives you fresh eyes that enable you to see errors you might not notice when you're in a hurry to send an email.

- Find a buddy and request a peer review. No. We're not saying you should be showing every email you write to a colleague. What we're saying is that for a high-stakes email, like a marketing message or fund-raising letter, you should consider asking a trusted coworker to proofread that communication before you send it.

When you've given your message one last objective review and are sure it's error free, then, and only then, click "Send."

Risks/Consequences

Inaccurate information can cause countless problems, from embarrassment and poor decision making to serious safety or legal issues. Plus, content errors cause you to lose credibility with the reader, or your company could be negatively affected due to dissemination of inaccurate information.

And, if you think convention errors aren't that important, think again. You might believe that only your English teachers cared and that losing a few points on an assignment wasn't that big of a deal. Maybe not. But in business, the stakes can be high. Poor use of language usually results in

- Confusion
- Misunderstanding

- Lost credibility
- Annoyed readers
- Humorous messages (humorous to readers, but NOT to you, the writer)

Errors in business communication can cost organizations money—a lot of money. The following examples demonstrate that errors can result in jeering and joking, yes, but such errors can also result in severe financial consequences.

- The tickets for a State of the Union address were printed with an error: the final word, which should have been "Union," appeared as "Uniom." The tickets were reprinted to correct the errors (at an undetermined cost to taxpayers).

- In Oneida County New York, voter ballots were printed with a candidate's name misspelled (*Barak* instead of *Barack*), costing the county over $75,000.

- A medical publication listed a therapist's occupation as "the rapist," setting the stage for a libel suit. That may have been a very expensive extra space.

- The Pacific Bell Yellow Pages described a travel agency's destinations as "erotic" instead of "exotic." This error resulted in the agency being awarded more than $19 million for the irreversible damage to its professional reputation and loss of customers due to the misprint.

The bottom line is that convention errors go beyond just being simple mistakes that are embarrassing; they can become a financial liability. You'll make mistakes; we all do. Using strategies to foster error-free communication, though, will **significantly reduce** the number of mistakes in your emails.

Error Free Scan

Abby knows she must care about correctness. To make sure her message is error free, she scans for inaccurate content and convention errors.

Misaligned Message with Error Free Diagnosis

TO: Chris Martinez
FROM: Abby Shultz
DATE: October 1, 2022
SUBJECT: RE: Request to Attend Conference

Hi Chris,

I appreciate your interest in attending the *We're Wired* IT conference—staying current in our industry is important to both your professional development and our department's goals.

Because we encourage employees *[missing punctuation]* continuing education, our department budgeted $10K for professional development in 2022, however, *[incorrect punctuation]* due to the high volume of applications and approvals since January, only $500 remain available. *[subject-verb agreement error]*

I'd be glad to discuss alternitives *[spelling error]* that would help you prepare for the software updates such as
- Attending the virtual option of the *We're Wired* conference
- Completing a vendor-provided online training program
- Securing the remaining conference costs from other sources listed in the <u>HR Professional Development</u> folder

I want to make sure we secure that $500 for you;   *[spacing error]* so, let me know by September 5 *[inaccurate date]* if you'd like to meet to discuss you're *[incorrect word]* options.

Thanks for taking initiative regarding your continuing professional development.

Best,
Abby

Abby Shultz, PMP
Director of Operations
DK Solutions
444.555.4321 // Direct

Error Free Adjustments

Observe Abby's adjustments, which correct inaccurate information, grammar/
spelling/punctuation mistakes, typos, and format errors.

Properly Aligned Message with Error Free Adjustments

TO: Chris Martinez
FROM: Abby Shultz
DATE: October 1, 2022
SUBJECT: RE: Request to Attend Conference

Hi Chris,

I appreciate your interest in attending the *We're Wired* IT conference—staying
current in our industry is important to both your professional development and our
department's goals.

Because we encourage employees' [*apostrophe indicates plural possessive: to
whom the continuing education belongs—all employees*] continuing education,
our department budgeted $10K for professional development in 2022. However,
[*run-on sentence corrected with a period between the two sentences and
starting the second sentence with a capital "H"*] due to the high volume of
applications and approvals since January, only $500 remains available. [*grammar
error corrected: $500 is a collective noun and requires the verb "remains" for
subject/verb agreement*]

I'd be glad to discuss alternatives [*spelling error corrected*] that would help you
prepare for the software updates such as
 • Attending the virtual option of the *We're Wired* conference
 • Completing a vendor-provided online training program
 • Securing the remaining conference costs from other sources listed in the <u>HR
    Professional Development</u> folder

I want to make sure we secure that $500 for you; [*spacing corrected, leaving only
one space after the semicolon*] so, let me know by October 5 [date corrected] if
you'd like to meet to discuss your [*word corrected: "your" (possessive) instead of
"you're," which is the contraction for "you are"*] options.

Thanks for taking initiative regarding your continuing professional development.

Best,
Abby

Abby Shultz, PMP
Director of Operations
DK Solutions
444.555.4321 // Direct

Abby's adjusted message is a more accurate reflection of her professionalism. Because she values her readers as well as her image, she knows she needs to send an error-free message.

Errors can interfere with a message's effectiveness. Don't make your readers search for some kind of email adapter to figure out how to read your written communication. When editing and proofreading your messages, check for inaccurate content, convention errors, and typos.

Remember, you're often judged by your writing. When written communication contains any kind of error, readers might assume you are careless, lazy, apathetic, sloppy, unprofessional, not credible, etc. You don't want any of these descriptors attributed to you! Conversely, error-free documents convey that you're professional, capable, conscientious, and credible—that you have BACKBONE!

Error Free BACKBONE Adjustments: What to Check Before You Click "Send"

• Accuracy—information, names, dates, numbers
• Correct Use of Conventions—grammar, spelling, punctuation, etc.

Okay, people, you now have the power to create messages with communication BACKBONE. Take your newly acquired email moxie (spunk, confidence, and skill) and start sending messages that get stuff done.

But wait . . . there's more!

Appendix

What Now?

Thought you'd finished the book, didn't you? Well, not so fast! This appendix includes some other vital communication signs we'd like you to monitor as the savvy email writer you've become.

To help keep a finger on the pulse of your communication wellness, pay attention to the following important message about pronouns, Cathy's abridged treatise on the writing process, and one of Lynna's many handy checklists—each packed with email essentials designed to support your communication power.

Pronouns: The Double Play That Takes Out Nouns

Being confused about what pronoun you should use is understandable for two reasons. First, English grammar is complicated, which causes frustration and apathy. Second, language changes over time, and as you may have noticed, the way we use pronouns has changed significantly in the last few years. So, if you're not sure what pronoun to use, you're not alone.

How we refer to our fellow humans is important, especially in writing. As professionals, we want to demonstrate competent communication and respect for those to whom, and about whom, we write. So pronouns matter.

A pronoun is a word used to substitute for a noun or noun phrase in order to avoid repeating that noun or noun phrase in a sentence. (See the irony here?) Some common pronouns are *her, him,* and *them.*

> Without a pronoun:
> **Diana** *is going to redevelop our website, and I'm going to help* **Diana***.*
> With a pronoun:
> **Diana** *is going to redevelop our website, and I'm going to help* **her***.*

In the second example, "Diana" is replaced by "her." When a pronoun such as "her" substitutes for a noun, that noun is then referred to as the "antecedent." Grammatically speaking, pronouns should agree with their antecedents in

- number (meaning singular or plural)
- gender (meaning male or female)

In the second example above, "Diana" is one person (singular) and female, so using the pronoun "her" to show agreement, in number and gender, with the antecedent "Diana" makes sense and is correct. But communicating with people isn't always that clear or binary because you may not know where they identify on the gender spectrum.

You may have seen email signatures that include a list of the sender's preferred pronouns such as *he, him, his, she, her, hers* or *they, them, their.* The three different pronouns in these examples are used depending on how they function in a sentence—whether they are subjective *(he/she/they),* objective *(him/her/them),* or possessive *(his/hers/their).* But this is not a grammar book, so here's what you need to know, right now, about being a respectful, inclusive communicator and following current guidelines for pronoun use.

> Without a pronoun:
> *The* **facilities director** *developed a process for international shipping that the* **facilities director** *will make available to employees on July 1.*

Using a pronoun as a substitute for the noun "facilities director" when it is used the second time reduces repetition. In the following example, the facilities director is male or prefers male pronouns:

> *The **facilities director** developed a process for international shipping that **he** will make available to employees on July 1.*

If the facilities director is female or prefers female pronouns, you could write this:

> *The **facilities director** developed a process for international shipping that **she** will make available to employees on July 1.*

Of course, if there are two facilities directors, use "they" (the plural regardless of their genders):

> *The **facilities directors** developed a process for international shipping that **they** will make available to employees on July 1.*

But what if there is just one facilities director and you don't know where that person identifies on the gender spectrum or what pronouns they prefer? Should you use "his or her" or "his/her" as a way to get around not knowing someone's gender? No—those are very clunky and space-consuming alternatives; plus, they are not gender inclusive.

If you're uncertain about the facility director's gender or don't know their preferred pronoun, it's perfectly fine to use the newly accepted conventions for pronoun and antecedent agreement and write "they" to refer to a singular "facilities director."

> *The **facilities director** developed a process for international shipping that **they** will make available to employees on July 1.*

Alternatively, you might consider using more progressive—although not necessarily new—options for gender neutral pronouns. For example, the following can be used if you don't want to assume a gender for the person or persons being referred to: "ze, zir, zirs" or "xe, xem, xirs." If those sound odd to you, consider getting over it—language evolves. You may not need to use "xirs" yet, but be prepared to incorporate gender-neutral pronoun practices into your workplace writing.

How to Get from Here to Send: Everything You Always Wanted to Know About the Email Writing Process but Were Afraid to Ask

An email message is a product you create through mental and physical effort; it's an official record of communication generated through a series of steps—a process. And as with many processes you practice regularly, such as brushing your teeth, you may complete the steps of writing an email without really giving them much thought. But we assure you, those steps *are* worth thinking about.

Take, for example, that nutritious smoothie you drink to fuel up for a workout or hike. That smoothie doesn't just appear when you think about it. Before you can enjoy that smoothie, you have to think about making it, prepare to make it, and then actually make it: you decide what flavor you want, assemble and measure the ingredients, put everything into the blender, put the top on the blender, and then turn the blender on, then off. And sometimes you make adjustments during that process based on your observations of the smoothie's color, texture, or taste. That multi-step process yields a singular, synthesized product—your delicious smoothie.

Similarly, writing a healthy email message requires a process, and even, perhaps, some adjustments based on observations along the way. Nobody expects—nor should you—a workplace email to appear magically, ready to send. Nor will it cascade carelessly from your brain and through your fingers onto the screen, perfectly organized and executed, without any planning or process following on your part. To end up with a well-written, synthesized message, you must carry out a series of steps. As you read the following, keep in mind that short, routine emails may require very little planning while longer, more difficult emails may involve extensive planning.

Typically, the writing process comprises three primary stages completed in this order: plan, draft, and edit. Further, each stage includes a few internal steps; some of those steps take merely a few seconds or minutes, depending on the complexity of the message. What follows is our BACKBONE-supporting process for writing spectacular email messages.

Stage One: Think and Plan

Steps:

1. Establish your purpose. Put into words what you want to accomplish through writing the message (**B**icentric).
2. Determine and analyze your audience. Identify what readers need to know and how they'll benefit (**B**icentric and **K**een).
3. Gather any information you need to write a complete message (**N**ourished).
4. Make mental or written notes. Start organizing thoughts as you prepare to write, and generate a list or outline of what ideas to include in the message, paying attention to how that content should be organized (**O**rdered).

Warning—if you skip this stage, you're putting your communication wellbeing at risk. Planning may take one minute. Or, depending on the complexity of the email, you may need a few days to think through the message, gather information, or discuss the subject with others. But planning, no matter how long it takes, will save you time later **and** will help you produce a better message. Complete this stage in your head, with voice notes, or in writing. Just do it.

Stage Two: Draft and Revise
Steps:

1. Write a complete draft of the message using your outline (or whatever you created during the planning stage) as a guide. Even if you're not sure how to begin, putting something on the screen in plain, conversational language will give you confidence; the more text you generate, the more you'll have to work with. And having something to work with is always easier than having nothing.

2. Revise, which literally means "to see again," and adjust your message, making changes to the large communication muscle groups, such as purpose, audience, content, and organization.

3. Read your working draft objectively, making sure that, overall, it accomplishes its purpose and is catered specifically to its intended audience.

Stage Three: Edit and Proofread
Steps:

1. Edit the message—make changes to its epidermis, or outer layer, to fix or improve any imperfections so that the message makes the impression you want to convey and uses correct conventions. Make sure it's clear, as concise as it can be, uses an appropriate tone, and incorporates a conversational style (**A**ssertive, **C**lear, and **B**uff).

2. Take a quick break and do something else for a while so you can return to the message with a fresh perspective and some objectivity before you take one final look.

3. Proofread your message. Use one or more of the following strategies for proofreading depending on the email's length, your workspace situation, and the techniques that work best for you (**Error Free**):

   • Take an additional break before you read your message again.

   • Read your message slowly, out loud, or vocalize it quietly.

   • Ask someone else to proofread it for you.

   • Read it backwards, which takes everything out of context and forces you to look at individual items or small chunks of text objectively.

After looking at the three stages, you may have noticed that reading, reviewing, and revising are built into the writing process. You may be getting the impression that writing isn't as straightforward as it looks. And you're right.

Typing letters and watching them turn into words as they appear from left to right across your screen looks linear (like a line). But seeing those lines stack up and the resulting feeling of productivity is misleading; in practice, you type for a while and then go back to read what you've written, creating a sort of writing and reading loop. The longer the message, the more loops of varying sizes you make. This looping motion is called recursive; it's a series of cycles of writing and then reading what you've written and then writing again. Use the recursiveness of the process to your advantage—embrace it. It takes the pressure off of trying to find every mistake or typo in one read through.

So why should you consider all of this when you just want to write a simple email? Because not all emails are created equally—each one is going to be unique based on purpose, audience, content, length, etc. But if you follow the suggested process and find a routine that works for you, you can tweak that process and write any email you need to create.

Using the same writing routine for all your messages reduces the risk you'll leave something out, send a message that's unclear or includes mistakes, or have to spend time putting on your virtual rubber gloves to clean up a workplace communication hazard. Your email writing routine will become comfortable, pliable, and strong and will support your every email writing need.

And to assist you with all of your email writing needs, be sure to use the BACKBONE Adjustments Checklist—no extra charge!

BACKBONE Adjustments: What to Check Before You Click "Send"

Bicentric
• Purpose—clearly stated and focused
• Audience—attends to reader's needs and possible reactions

Assertive
• Tone—positive words and phrasing; states what can be done
• Style—confident, courteous, and sincere

Clear
• Word Choice—appropriate for reader and context; conversational style
• Sentences—fewer than 20 words each
• Fluency—transitions incorporated; sentence structure varied
• Readability—easy to read and only one way to interpret
• Design Techniques—effective use of white space and graphic highlighting

Keen
• "You" Attitude—considers reader's needs and wants; includes reader benefits
• Nondiscriminatory Language—free of sexist and biased language
• Enthusiastic Style—conveys energy
• Word Choice—precise, concrete, and correct

Buff
• Relevant Information—unnecessary information removed
• Conversational Style—as you'd speak to that audience, in that situation
• Conciseness—only words that add value are included
• Active Voice—80 percent of sentences (subject does the action on the verb)

Ordered
• Beginning:
  Subject Line—signal words and do-know statement
  Greeting—appropriate level of formality
  First Sentence—positive note that is sincere and related to the message
• Middle:
  Length—maximum of five short paragraphs
  Information—presented in a logical order
  Appropriate Organizational Pattern—direct or indirect
• End:
  Friendly Ending—genuine and tailored to the message
  Sign-off—appropriate level of formality
  Signature—appropriate for message formality and relationship with reader

Nourished
• Complete—all necessary information included
• Supplemented (if applicable)—visuals, hyperlinks, attachments

Error Free
• Accuracy—information, names, dates, numbers
• Correct Use of Conventions—grammar, spelling, punctuation, etc.

CPSIA information can be obtained
at www.ICGtesting.com
Printed in the USA
JSHW012302110623
42987JS00003B/84